T0087323

I Do! I Do!

VOCAL SELECTION

Book & Lyrics by

TOM JONES

Music by

HARVEY SCHMIDT

based on "The Fourposter" by Jan de Hartog

Contents

	page
I Do! I Do!	4
I Love My Wife	8
The Honeymoon Is Over	12
Where Are The Snows?	18
Together Forever	24
What Is A Woman?	27
Someone Needs Me	30
Roll Up The Ribbons	34
My Cup Runneth Over	37
This House	42

Purchase of this vocal score does not entitle the purchaser to perform the work in public. All rights including public performances for profit are reserved to the authors. For information regarding performances of the work write to:

MUSIC THEATRE INTERNATIONAL
545 8th Avenue, New York, N.Y. 10018

TOM JONES   HARVEY SCHMIDT

Tom Jones and Harvey Schmidt began writing musical comedies when they were both students at the University of Texas. Later on, in New York, they wrote revue material for Julius Monk's Upstairs-Downstairs and Ben Bagley's "Shoestring Revues." In May, 1960, Lore Noto produced Jones and Schmidt's "The Fantasticks" at the Sullivan Street Playhouse where it has become the longest running musical production ever to play on or off Broadway.

Their first Broadway effort was "110 In The Shade," a musical based on N. Richard Nash's "The Rainmaker." "110" was greeted favorably in New York with the critics particularly singling out the score for praise. Most recently Mary Martin and Robert Preston have set Broadway aflame with Jones and Schmidt's musicalization of Jan de Hartog's comedy "The Fourposter" entitled "I Do! I Do!" Directed by Gower Champion, "I Do! I Do!" has become the latest theatrical triumph for Tom Jones and Harvey Schmidt.

I Do! I Do!

Presented by DAVID MERRICK. First performance
December 5, 1966 at the Forty-Sixth Street Theatre, New York

Directed by GOWER CHAMPION

Scenic Production Oliver Smith
Costumes by Freddy Wittop
Lighting by Jean Rosenthal
Musical Direction by John Lesko
Orchestrations by Philip J. Lang
Assistant to the Director Lucia Victor

A DAVID MERRICK AND CHAMPION-SIX, INC. PRODUCTION

Cast of Characters

(In order of appearance)

SHE (*Agnes*) . . . . MARY MARTIN
HE (*Michael*) . . . . ROBERT PRESTON

Duo pianists Woody Kessler, Albert Mello

Scenic Synopsis

THE TIME
The story covers fifty years of a marriage,
beginning just before the turn of the century.

THE PLACE
A Bedroom

Original Cast Album by RCA Victor

I Do, I Do

Words by
TOM JONES

Music by
HARVEY SCHMIDT

There's a strange new world that you en - ter when you say: I

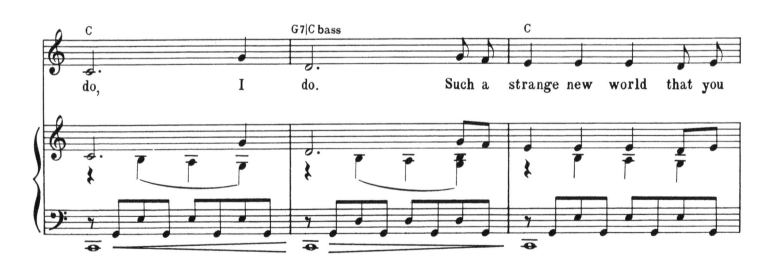

do, I do. Such a strange new world that you

Copyright © 1966 by Tom Jones & Harvey Schmidt
Portfolio Music, Inc. & Chappell & Co., Inc., Administrators of publication and allied rights throughout the World.
International Copyright Secured   ALL RIGHTS RESERVED   Printed in the U.S.A.
Unauthorized copying, arranging, adapting, recording or public performance is an infringement of copyright.
Infringers are liable under the law.

I Love My Wife

Words by
TOM JONES

Music by
HARVEY SCHMIDT

Copyright © 1966 by Tom Jones & Harvey Schmidt
Portfolio Music, Inc. & Chappell & Co., Inc., Administrators of publication and allied rights throughout the World.
International Copyright Secured   ALL RIGHTS RESERVED   Printed in the U.S.A.
Unauthorized copying, arranging, adapting, recording or public performance is an infringement of copyright.
Infringers are liable under the law.

Oth- er men love *Femme Fa-tales,* Svelte - ly dressed; But when I'm with those femme fa -tales I get de - pressed; 'cause I love my wife. How will it end? I love her as a lov - er and not just as a friend. It

The Honeymoon Is Over

Words by
TOM JONES

Music by
HARVEY SCHMIDT

Copyright © 1966 by Tom Jones & Harvey Schmidt
Portfolio Music, Inc. & Chappell & Co., Inc., Administrators of publication and allied rights throughout the World.
International Copyright Secured   ALL RIGHTS RESERVED   Printed in the U.S.A.
Unauthorized copying, arranging, adapting, recording or public performance is an infringement of copyright.
Infringers are liable under the law.

Where Are The Snows?

Words by
TOM JONES

Music by
HARVEY SCHMIDT

Copyright © 1966 by Tom Jones & Harvey Schmidt
Portfolio Music, Inc. & Chappell & Co., Inc., Administrators of publication and allied rights throughout the World.
International Copyright Secured   ALL RIGHTS RESERVED   Printed in the U.S.A.
Unauthorized copying, arranging, adapting, recording or public performance is an infringement of copyright.
Infringers are liable under the law.

"I DO! I DO!" MARY MARTIN

Do! **ROBERT PRESTON** ♡♡ **I DO! I DO!** ♡♡

Together Forever

Words by
TOM JONES

Music by
HARVEY SCHMIDT

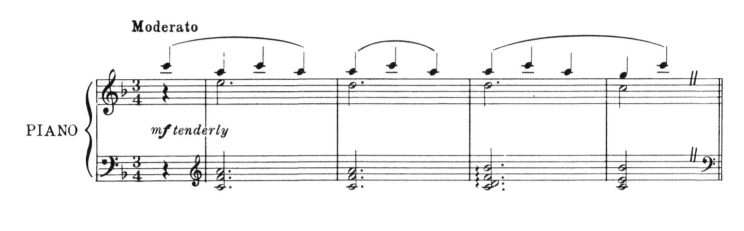

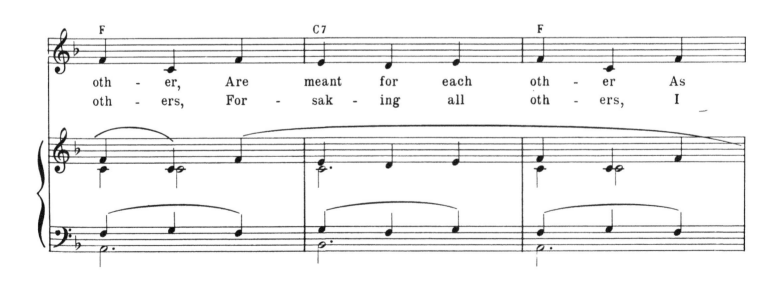

Copyright © 1966 by Tom Jones & Harvey Schmidt
Portfolio Music, Inc. & Chappell & Co., Inc., Administrators of publication and allied rights throughout the World.
International Copyright Secured   ALL RIGHTS RESERVED   Printed in the U.S.A.
Unauthorized copying, arranging, adapting, recording or public performance is an infringement of copyright.
Infringers are liable under the law.

"*I Do, I Do*"

What Is A Woman?

Words by
TOM JONES

Music by
HARVEY SCHMIDT

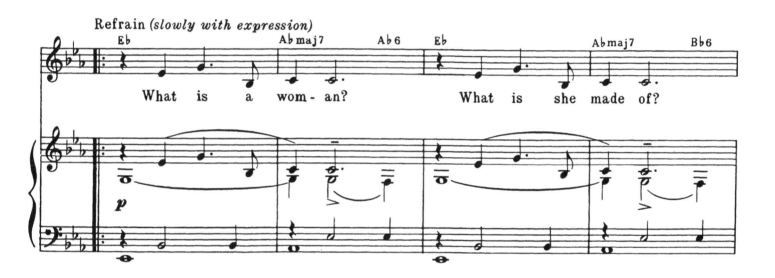

Copyright © 1966 by Tom Jones & Harvey Schmidt
Portfolio Music, Inc. & Chappell & Co., Inc., Administrators of publication and allied rights throughout the World.
International Copyright Secured   ALL RIGHTS RESERVED   Printed in the U.S.A.
Unauthorized copying, arranging, adapting, recording or public performance is an infringement of copyright.
Infringers are liable under the law.

Someone Needs Me

Words by
TOM JONES

Music by
HARVEY SCHMIDT

Copyright © 1966 by Tom Jones & Harvey Schmidt
Portfolio Music, Inc. & Chappell & Co., Inc., Administrators of publication and allied rights throughout the World.
International Copyright Secured   ALL RIGHTS RESERVED   Printed in the U.S.A.
Unauthorized copying, arranging, adapting, recording or public performance is an infringement of copyright.
Infringers are liable under the law.

Roll Up The Ribbons

Words by
TOM JONES

Music by
HARVEY SCHMIDT

Copyright © 1966 by Tom Jones & Harvey Schmidt
Portfolio Music, Inc. & Chappell & Co., Inc., Administrators of publication and allied rights throughout the World.
International Copyright Secured   ALL RIGHTS RESERVED   Printed in the U.S.A.
Unauthorized copying, arranging, adapting, recording or public performance is an infringement of copyright.
Infringers are liable under the law.

"I Do, I Do"

My Cup Runneth Over

Words by
TOM JONES

Music by
HARVEY SCHMIDT

Copyright © 1966 by Tom Jones & Harvey Schmidt
Portfolio Music, Inc. & Chappell & Co., Inc., Administrators of publication and allied rights throughout the World.
International Copyright Secured   ALL RIGHTS RESERVED   Printed in the U.S.A.
Unauthorized copying, arranging, adapting, recording or public performance is an infringement of copyright.
Infringers are liable under the law.

This House

Words by
TOM JONES

Music by
HARVEY SCHMIDT

Copyright © 1966 by Tom Jones & Harvey Schmidt
Portfolio Music, Inc. & Chappell & Co., Inc., Administrators of publication and allied rights throughout the World.
International Copyright Secured   ALL RIGHTS RESERVED   Printed in the U.S.A.
Unauthorized copying, arranging, adapting, recording or public performance is an infringement of copyright.
Infringers are liable under the law.